390 WIS
Wisdom, Emma J.   ANF
A practical guide to planning a

A Practical Guide to

Planning A
Family Reunion

by

Emma J. Wisdom

A Practical Guide to Planning a Family Reunion

© Copyright 1988, Emma J. Wisdom. All rights reserved.

No part of this book may be reproduced without the permission of the publisher. Address inquiries to Post Oak Publications.

ISBN 0-9620115-0-9
Library of Congress 88-090539

Printed in the United States of America.

Illustrated by Mary Elizabeth Townsel
Cover design by JM Productions

Published by:
Post Oak Publications
P.O. Box 8455
Nashville, TN 37207-0455

Anything conceivable

and believable

is achievable.

— Anonymous

ACKNOWLEDGMENTS

As no book is the product of one individual, several people have helped in one way or another to enable me to complete this guide. And I wish to thank the following people for contributing their time, information, materials, suggestions, talents, and skills while I was writing this book: Karen Brown, Debra Malone Coleman, Mattie B. Davis, Debbie Jones, Audrey Hall, Roxie Johnson, Emma Marie Osborne, Douglas Paschall, Timothy Spence, Mary M. Vowels, Linda Crook Williams, Jessie Wilson, and Mary Yarbrough.

Table of Contents

To my family.

AUTHOR'S NOTES

Writing this book developed naturally out of planning a reunion for my family and helping to organize numerous other reunions for friends. This book was equally written in answer to the many questions which have been posed to me over the years. Responses and explanations regarding queries about issues of money, menus, correspondence, and publicity, to things like housing, contacting distant relatives, and coordinating fun activities, to arranging for photographers and musicians have been developed carefully.

Many brainstorming sessions and collective ideas have been cultivated from my own experiences and from many generous people who have graciously shared their ideas with me. And from these success stories, I have gleaned the best gems to show you how to approach the planning phase if you've never organized a family reunion before. Or, if you have, you'll probably find new ideas and activities you'll like to include. This book was written as much for the novice as for the veteran planner, who both may be looking for the best way to "re-union" with family and close friends.

While this book is designed primarily as a guide to planning a family reunion, its usefulness is not limited. Church groups, social clubs, class reunion organizers, military veterans, professional organizations, and small businesses will find it helpful in organizing gatherings or conventions. Many of the details are easily translatable to other functions. The chapter on budgeting might be of particular interest. How to work effectively with newspapers and other media in publicizing an event is another area of great concern where you will find tips to smooth the way. I've mentioned only three of these. There are many others adaptable to your needs.

This guide has been divided into three primary coordinating areas to help you each step along in this exciting family venture: conceiving the idea for a family reunion, believing in its success, and achieving what you set out to do.

And finally this book has been written for "you" — the thousands of people who feel as strongly as I do about maintaining family ties. To you I feel a kinship, and I hope this guide will show you how to plan the best family reunion or gathering possible — one which will be long remembered.

INTRODUCTION

The publication of Alex Haley's *Roots* in 1976 and its television sequel a year later whetted the appetite of millions of people in America and around the globe to delve into the fascinating discovery of family heritage.

A beginning to your trek to connect your present pedigree to generations past is the family reunion. The family reunion is one way you can learn about your ancestry. You can start here to gather bits and pieces of facts from family members by one-on-one contact, of course, or bring the clan together in a group setting for a family reunion and get many of the facts you will need first hand.

But, if you are like most people, you have probably kept in touch with a small handful of relatives. And almost all of us have asked a similar question — "Whatever happened to Cousin Grace or Uncle Joe?" The possibility of making connection with a lost relative or of having a family reunion begins to take shape in your mind and then ferments and grows. Maybe. So you check your family sources to help you contact a number of lost kin that you had only given occasional thought to before *Roots*. Perhaps you timidly or confidently believe they can help bring your personal dream to fruition.

Then you toss the idea around in your head for days and for some reason you just never get around to doing anything about it. You think it's a great idea; you want to do it; but after mentioning it to one or two relatives you find they are interested but the time is bad for them to help in the preparation. They leave it to you to take the lead and coordinate the entire affair, if it's to take place at all. They commit themselves only to attending such an occasion.

After calculating the time involved in contacting the entire family by phone or letter, you realize that the whole thing could be very time-consuming. Besides, who has the time to find relatives who have dropped out of the family circle? Where will all these people stay? What kind of menu would be suitable for the occasion? Who will do the cooking? On the other hand, should the food be catered? What about the children — how will they be entertained while the grownups are "reunioning"? Where should the reunion be held — at Uncle Joe's or at Aunt Clara's place, or mom's and dad's place? Or would a state park be better?

Finally, you say forget it. It would take a fine-tuned army and a drill sergeant to pull off a family reunion.

Admittedly, there will be lots of planning and organizing to do. Also in planning a family reunion, you will confront doubters and nay-sayers, no-shows, and a host of other unnerving little incidents before the big day. But you'll find that, in retrospect, there's no describing the joy and oneness you feel the day of the reunion; the feeling of belonging and self-identity, of love, caring, and friendship; the feeling of a healing effect and wellness; and, of course, a sense of history.

There are two kinds of commonly thought-of family reunions: one is repeated on a regular basis when you rejoin your spouse and children or your mom and dad at home after a day at school, work, or leisure. Or, it could be one that is held periodically when you visit mom and dad, aunts and uncles, or sisters and brothers, grandparents and other relatives on weekends. Of course, the other or more formal kind of family reunion is when you have been separated for a longer time period and reunite, as is the case with the typical all-family reunion. It's when third or fourth cousins removed, aunts and uncles, sisters and brothers, mothers and fathers, in-laws, and others connected to the family travel from short distances or from afar to visit the original home place or some other special place on an appointed date and time.

The family reunion we will be discussing throughout this book is the kind which meets once a year, every other year, every three years, every five or ten years, or even for the very first time. It's the one which takes time to plan and is structured to get the most out of the time the family spends together. It could be the old-fashioned kind; it could just as well be a one-day occasion; it could include two or even three days of activities on land none of the family has ever been to before or on the family's original home place. The site isn't the most important detail. In fact, the most important thing is reuniting with family members. Everything else is secondary.

When my aunt and I were planning our family reunion four years ago, we managed to completely plan the event just narrowly within the time frame generally necessary: it took six months to synchronize a one-day occasion, which did not occur without some unplanned events. All in all, it was a fine day indeed, and we had to admit we had fun planning it. Our expectations were exceeded tenfold on all fronts from beginning to ending. Everyone seemed to enjoy the day thoroughly. I am still receiving favorable responses from those who attended. Relatives are still asking us when we are going to have the next one.

At almost every juncture along the way — at the print shop, at the trophy and plaque shop, with the artist drawing the specially designed T-shirts, with the caterers, with the photographers — invariably someone would comment that they were planning a family reunion, just recently attended one, or thought what we were doing was a great idea. Yet some admitted they personally had been unable to get one off the ground for their own family. There were also many inquiries about just how to plan one, and this guide is the outgrowth of such questions posed to us during the course of planning our reunion and my assistance in the planning of others.

To have a family reunion, one or two persons or as many as four or six can do the planning; the number depends on how many days or how elaborate the affair will be. Ideally, the planners should live nearby, but it can be done from distant locations; that is, if you don't mind corresponding through the mail or higher phone bills. In the case of my own family reunion, the whole affair was planned by two people from two different states, with family members agreeing to participate as tasks were identified. One family's reunion had eleven members on the team. Another family's reunion involved nine people in coordinating events and still another recruited ten people to work on planning their events.

If you have been thinking about having a family reunion or even researching your family heritage as Alex Haley and many others have done, you, too, will find that it is not impossible to do, and you'll have fun doing it. And above all, it may be just the shot in the arm to bring distant relatives back into the fold. (They were probably waiting for the opportune time to return, anyway. A family reunion can be the avenue they were looking and hoping for to break the ice.) If I have whetted your appetite to plan a reunion and you have decided to go ahead, this guide will give you information, suggestions, and forms to use in planning your family reunion.

Careful planning is the key to a great family reunion. You *can* do it. Find a few willing bodies to help get started. It is guaranteed to be a memorable occasion to add to your family annals. I even bet a lot of your relatives will thank you for taking the initiative. Keep in mind, however, that there is no one way to plan a family reunion. Rather, there are as many ways as there are innovative and creative ideas and families. Use your best judgment, seek ideas from your planners and go with what is best for your particular situation and will give the family the best time together. Afterwards you may even be ready to take on being the first one in the family to go a step further and trace your roots.

Part I

Conceiving the Idea

Anything conceivable...

CHAPTER 1

TALK IT OVER – AND – UP

If you are the person who suggests a family reunion, be prepared to volunteer your time or even to act as the coordinator of the entire event. Are you ready to take on such a role? No need to answer just yet. First things first.

Who and What

Call around to several members of the family who live nearby to see if you can draw enough interest in having a family reunion, because you will need the full cooperation of the majority of your relatives to carry out such an occasion. You will also need three or four people to serve as core planners. But don't expect everyone you contact to be as enthusiastic about the idea as perhaps you are at this point. You may have to bring them around. Be prepared to do this if you feel strongly enough about the idea. It might require a bit of a selling job to convince them. Also, listen carefully to their responses when you first introduce your idea. Although they may not be willing to participate in the planning phase, you still want them to attend.

When and Where

There's usually one member of the family who has kept up with what is happening with everyone and their whereabouts. Check with that person. A date for the reunion can be planned around an event such as an upcoming wedding or wedding anniversary celebration or baby christening.

Family members usually attend these special occasions. Although these particular events may include more of one immediate branch of the family than another, there is a good possibility that others will attend as well. If it is possible to keep any one family member from traveling a long distance to attend, you should consider what an added trip could cause in financial and timing hardships.

Since many people take vacations during the summer months or around holidays, these dates are probably the best times to have a reunion. Memorial Day, Independence Day (Fourth of July), and Labor Day all seem to fit most people's schedule and are great for large outdoor gatherings. Good Friday, Easter, Mother's Day or Father's Day, Thanksgiving, Christmas, or New Year's holidays are dates not out of the question. Just be considerate of others' available time and when you think you will get the largest number in attendance. Then pick the date(s) and place. And go with it!

If you already have some idea of the place that family members would love to visit, this might be the opportune time to arrange such a trip. Whether a distant location or the original homesite, just make sure it's a location reasonably accessible to the entire family.

How Much Will It Cost?

You may only know at the moment that you wish to have a family reunion. But the kinds of activities you plan will have a significant impact on the cost of the reunion. And soon after it becomes known that there is sufficient interest generated among family members to keep the idea alive, you will need to give some thought to the kinds of activities which will be involved, the number of days the reunion will last, and so forth.

When setting the dates, give equal time to considering events.

Much of this can be done by the core planners, but it certainly will need to be done before any notifications are sent to relatives. For instance, is it going to be a three-day affair — Friday, Saturday, and Sunday? The first day may include a formal dinner and fashion show; the second day may be an informal picnic with games and prizes; and the third day, the family may attend a memorial service together.

These are only a few of the many details you must decide in planning any kind of get-together such as a family reunion. Ideas for family reunion activities and events, along with developing a budget, will be discussed in more detail in later chapters.

Plus Persuasion

If there's the slightest hint or doubt from the initial contact made with relatives, now may be a good time to send out a "feeler" or "convincer" kind of correspondence to pique interest and to persuade them rather than an announcement of the family reunion. It just depends upon your particular family. But if you have doubters and a slow-to-come-around-to-an-idea kind of family, your best bet is to check out the climate before you've gone too far along with the planning phase. Whether it's a general announcement or a test run letter, get it out early, preferably six to twelve months before the proposed reunion date. The letters that follow will give you the general idea of what to include.

Dear _____,

Several of us have been talking about the Malones getting together for a family reunion next summer in Somerville — the kind where we plan to get together at a particular time on a happy occasion for a change.

Uncle Vernon, Aunt Clara, Debra, Lillie, Charles, LaDelle, and John all give thumbs up to the idea. What about the same response from you? What would you say to one of the following holiday weekends — Memorial Day, the Fourth of July, or Labor Day?

We're really excited about the possibility of all of us being in one place together. In order for the celebration to be a real family reunion, we need you to be there to "re-union" with us.

Just check off the items that apply on the enclosed card and return it to us here.

With Love and Affection,

Emma, Debra, and Those in
Favor of a Family Reunion

(See Chapter 5, Sending Announcements, for the acceptance form.)

When the votes have been counted and you get a go-ahead, follow up the first letter with the decision:

Dear _____,

The votes have been counted! Everyone agrees July 3, 4, and 5 is the best choice for a _____ Family Reunion. Mark your calendar! You don't want to miss what we are planning. We have already been busy lining up activities. Of course, we will keep in touch to inform you of the details.

In the meantime, please fill in the enclosed ACCEPTANCE form and return it to us as soon as possible.

With warm regards,

Dear _____,

We're planning a shootin', rootin', tootin' good time for you. It's going to be a real humdinger. We're letting you know early about the _____ Family Reunion on July 3, 4, and 5 so you can round up the lil twigs and big branches for a Tree Stomping Good Time. Just fill out the enclosed card and drop it in the mail, partner.

Y'all come, you hear. See you then! We'll be there,

With warm regards,

Calling Off a Family Reunion

Decide beforehand the number you'll need to go forward with your plans. If you don't get the minimum responses, call it off. Try again next year. The climate might be more favorable the second time around. But don't abandon the whole idea.

Dear _____,

Unfortunately, we didn't get the number we were hoping for to attend a _____ Family Reunion.

The July 3, 4, and 5 dates for a family reunion have been called off due to a lack of interest. Maybe next year.

Cordially,

Dear _____,

It seems by your response that it's not feasible to go ahead with plans for a _____ Family Reunion at this time. Therefore, July 3, 4, and 5 have been called off because of an insufficient number of favorable responses.

We'll try again next year.

Cordially,

PART II

ON WITH THE SHOW

Anything conceivable and believable...

CHAPTER 2

GETTING THINGS OFF THE GROUND

Now that the preliminaries have been taken care of and it's definite that your family wishes to have a reunion, you are ready to begin to put together a fantastic family reunion.

The first order of business is to call your core planners together. Don't make your core group more than four to six people. Any group larger than this usually means trouble and creates confusion, which has a tendency to delay progress. At this first meeting select your chair or coordinator, who will lead meetings thereafter. Select committee designations appropriate for the occasion being planned; for example, a coordinator, secretary, and treasurer. A person to chair housing, souvenirs, publicity and communications, banquet, picnic, or other committees can be added later, after your activities have taken shape and are more structured.

If your family is extremely large, and you are planning numerous activities, you may also wish to add an individual to coordinate each day's events. The coordinator of housing could decide which hotels will give the best choice of amenities for a certain block of rooms. Which company will design the T-shirts, sun visors, certificates, awards and plaques all may fall to the souvenir chair to work out.

When the time draws near, perhaps a publicity and communication committee will be the appropriate designation to communicate with the family. The secretary or another individual may be assigned this task. Writing the press release is another function that the coordinator of publicity and communications may be assigned to do as well. The bottom line in all of this is that all planning activities are coordinated through the core group.

The treasurer, of course, will collect the money to deposit in a bank account and pay all bills. This person should confer with a bank officer on the best kind of checking or savings account to open. It is also through the core group or planning committee that all activities will be reported.

Be sure that the secretary keeps notes of all decisions and actions taken. One group of family planners started their plans more than a year in advance. Here's a look at how one family began preparing for their reunion through a committee.

April 13, 1986

Meeting held at home of Emma Osborne.

Meeting was called to order by Emma Osborne. First order of business was the election of a chairperson. Emma Osborne was nominated. She was elected unanimously. Ruby Edmondson, vice chairperson; Sarah Johnson, treasurer; Patricia Allen, secretary. Dates approved for the reunion were July 17, 18, and 19, 1987 in Nashville.

The following committees were formed and their chairpersons are:

Site Committee, Oscar Hollinsworth

Organizational Committee, Thelma Scantling; members-- Deborah Goldthreate, Charles Demoss

T-shirt committee, Victoria Overton

These committees are to meet and be ready to report at the next meeting.

The next order of business was the paying of $10 fee each. This is due immediately to defray cost to mail information from meetings and to report progress.

Victoria made a motion that all mailings be held until after the next meeting. Charles seconded the motion. Motion carried.

Deborah made a motion that the meetings be held every fourth Sunday at 5 p.m. — seconded by Charles. Motion carried.

Victoria moved that the next meeting be held at the home of Charles on May 25 at 5 p.m. Motion was seconded and carried.

Meeting adjourned.

As you can discern from the initial meeting of these planners, several things were accomplished. Later, the recording of these actions will serve to refresh their memory of the decisions made. (This record is also an ideal way to provide a detailed, written history for future generations.) At this meeting, a chairperson, vice- chairperson, treasurer, secretary, as well as committees were named. Locations and dates were approved. Once officers and committees are in place, they will be expected to make reports at each meeting. And at subsequent meetings additional planning can fall into place, as is evident here. Though the planners altered these initial plans later, the basic framework was done at this meeting:

May 25, 1986

Meeting held at home of Charles Demoss.

Committee reports were given. Deborah suggested an agenda of activities for the weekend which was accepted by the group. They were as follows:

Friday — 6-9 p.m. — Cheese and wine sip social.

This will be a come and go affair. Time for everyone to meet and get acquainted.

Saturday — 10 a.m.-2 p.m. — Picnic

Saturday evening — Dance-Talent-Fashion Show

Sunday — Morning services at Gordon Memorial United Methodist Church

After these plans were accepted, the Organizational Committee led by Thelma Scantling was dissolved and became the Program Committee. It will be responsible for planning the actual activities, food, etc.

Treasurer's report made by Sarah Johnson. Money collected--$110. Expenditures included $10.67 used to pay for stationery which leaves a balance of $99.33.

Treasurer stated she needed a receipt book. Each member present gave $1 for a total of $8 to buy said book. Stamps will be purchased for out of town mailings.

The T-Shirt Committee suggested color schemes. The group voted and approved a yellow shirt with red lettering. Logo will be presented at the next meeting.

Meeting June 22, 1986, will be held at the home of Sarah Johnson at 5 p.m.

Meeting adjourned.

Before you get too involved, it's a good idea to form a "Things To Do Checklist" or work plan.

THINGS TO DO CHECKLIST

___1. List possible willing workers to make up planning team.

___2. Call a meeting to select coordinator, secretary, treasurer,and committees.

___3. Decide what kind of family reunion you wish to have.

___4. Set the date(s) and location.

___5. Decide on number of different events, i.e., get acquainted or arrival reception, picnic or backyard cookout, talent-fashion show, swap shop, banquet or dance, etc.

___6. Where will each activity be held? Will it be accessible to the hotel where most of the people will stay?

___7. Select a theme.

___8. Settle on a choice of one or two hotels. Reserve a block of rooms. (Estimate the number needed and firm up later.)

___9. Reserve hotel ballroom, civic hall, state park to hold events. (Details can be worked out later.) Set date to meet with convention representatives.

___10. Arrange a band to provide music. Set date to go over requirements with musicians.

___11. Decide on decorations.

___12. Order special souvenirs well in advance. (Games and prizes can be collected as you go along.)

___13. Engage additional people to act as helpers and servers, and as registrar.

___14. Hire limousines, vans and drivers to transport guests from hotel or homes to location of activities.

___15. Decide if reunion will be photographed and/or videotaped. Interview photographer and look over portfolio discriminately. Be sure person hired to videotape reunion has the technical knowledge needed.

___16. Open a savings or checking account depending upon your particular needs. (Explain this to the bank officer and follow his or her advice.)

__17. Arrange to pay expenses beforehand and as merchandise arrives or set up terms for services engaged.

__18. Arrange for a press release approximately six weeks before reunion, then follow up two weeks before activities.

__19. Follow up all agreements with a phone call or meeting to get specific information. Then confirm your understanding of details and cost in a letter. Enclose a copy and ask that it's signed and returned by a specific date.

__20. Purchase stationery, Thank You notes, a sufficient quantity of postage, index cards and a book for recording minutes. (You may need to purchase these items from personal monies until you build up a treasury.)

__21. Itemize all expenses. Then notify family members in your announcement communication the amount needed from each person or family to defray cost.

CHAPTER 3

STEPPING OUT

You will probably want to have at least one event during the family reunion that is a formal affair. It can be a talent show, a dinner dance, a fashion show (using relatives as models), or it may be a banquet where you make special presentations to the senior, the youngest, or the descendant who has been the most fruitful in the continuation of the family lineage, allowing five to ten minutes for impromptu remarks from family participants — a special touch such as I'M THANKFUL FOR _____, I AM _____ (briefly telling his or her linkage to the family group), or I AM HERE BECAUSE _____.

Here you might also give away other awards, plaques, and certificates that are appropriate for the occasion. For example, one lasting memento of the occasion is a certificate given to family participants. A certificate requires a modest outlay of money but gives the maximum return in appreciation from recipients. An individual will look at it and recall that special time in the family's history.

The design of a certificate can take many forms (see the following example). You can usually find shops which carry specialty items such as certificates, trophies, and plaques. Imprint them with sincerity and you'll have a real winning token.

If you decide on a full program, you will probably need a fashion coordinator and a moderator to preside over the evening. A small musical combo or band to provide suitable music during the meal and fashion

FLEMING - MALONE FAMILY REUNION

Gratefully Acknowledges and Appreciates

the

Attendance and Participation

of

_____

"WE ARE FAMILY"

July 7, 1985

Somerville, Texas

show is an added treat. Activities are usually performed by family participants. Are there musicians in the family? Can someone do justice to the moderator and presider spots? Talented individuals are found in most families. Don't be afraid to ask people what they do well.

Although you may have no problem in getting participants for the occasion, there are specifics you may want to consider. Individuals need not be professionals in these areas, merely willing to participate. Since you want things to go smoothly, select the best from your choices and move forward.

The Ma Jane Gardner Banquet and the Leath-Kage programs illustrate two family format choices (see Appendices B and C). Both show individuality. There is no right or wrong way to planning a family gathering. Do whatever will work for your family; providing fun and favorable memories should be the aim.

Hotels are usually accommodating to their guests for bringing them business. So, if you decide to have a formal occasion at a local hotel, ask about a courtesy suite, or if the banquet room comes free with your family room bookings. You will be surprised at what you can negotiate because of the number of reservations they get from an event being held there.

Is a picnic in the plans? If so, this could be the event where emphasis is placed on the children having fun. Most state parks have baseball fields, basketball courts, tennis courts, and areas for volleyball and swimming. Challenge the men to play the women and children at a baseball game; or with fathers against sons or mothers against daughters in any sport, you have the making for an hilarious time. Timing could not be better. It is a chance for the adults to show the children all their terrific school-day athletic moves — speed, agility, concentration, performance, etc. It is also a time for the youngsters to beat mom and dad in some sport in which they have excelled. It will be anyone's guess as to the outcome. But what fun it will be! A tug-of-war or a potato race are other options among many. Add any favorite family games and the mix will be just what is needed to cap off a perfect day of fun activities.

What if you decided to have a three-day family reunion? What events will be included each day? And if it is only for one day, what then? As you will see in Chapter 4 on establishing a budget, the outline shows three days which include a formal banquet or program, a picnic and family worship services together. Here are some suggestions of formats you might consider for your reunion.

Strike Up the Band

The banquet program can be as formal and elaborate as you wish. The only criterion is that it should be an organized and structured affair. Notice that the Ma Jane Gardner Family Reunion Planners (see Appendix B) decided on a program which included a hired band, a fashion show, and special presentations held on a Friday evening at a local hotel.

It was during the banquet that the occasion of the family reunion was given, with a brief history of how the reunion came about. Since the reunion was of two days' duration, the banquet was the kick-off event, which set the tone of the significance of their family gathering. Seven generations of matriarchal Jane Gardner were the focus. The family history was traced in the form of a tree with each child's branch noted or identified.

The planners of the Fleming-Malone Family Reunion (see Appendix A) decided on a Sunday for their big day because it seemed during several years of events they were only reunited during times of sad occasions — at the time of family illness or death. Even though the family, for the most part, lived within 200 miles of each other, they had not kept in touch on a regular basis. Rooted in a religious background, Sunday was the day chosen to reunite the matriarchal Fleming and patriarchal Malone families.

July 7, 1985 started with a continental breakfast in the Mount Calvary Baptist Church dining room that morning at nine o'clock, followed by worship service at 11 o'clock. Four generations from the Malone family and three generations from the Fleming family attended. The "occasion" message given by me near the beginning of the program highlighted the significance of the day. An excerpt of this part in the program is below:

In mid-1984, the idea to have a family reunion was discussed by Debra Malone Coleman and me.

From the beginning, our ultimate desire was to come together as a family unit on a happy occasion.

Celebration, family, reunion, descendant, heritage are words with significant meaning for each of us who has met in this place, on this day. The meanings that these words hold for us are descriptive and relevant because they summarize the purpose of our presence:

First, *celebrate* means "to commemorate an anniversary or holiday with festivity; to honor publicly; to have a good time."

Second, the word *family* is described as "a household; parents and children; all those descended from a common ancestor; lineage; a group of similar or related things."

Third, *reunion* is defined as "a coming together again, as after separation."

And next is *descendant*, which is "an offspring of a certain ancestor, family group, etc."

And last, *heritage.* Its meaning is "a tradition handed down from one's ancestors or the past."

So how then can we best characterize today's events? I believe that our presence here is symbolic, important, meaningful, and encompasses all of the above descriptions of *celebration, family, reunion, descendant, and heritage.*

This date, July 7, 1985, is our first such occasion to publicly honor loved ones whose spiritual presence is represented here through us and whose physical being will be remembered later during this morning's service. At the same time, we are also here to honor with cheer and praise the *living.*

We are here on this occasion to celebrate with festivity the unity of the Flemings and Malones and to have a good time together doing it.

"We Are Family." Each of us evolved from a household that began with a man and a woman into whose lives you and I entered at birth. And that union of man, woman, and child created a family of parents and child or a family of parents and children.

"We Are Family." We are of close bloodlines or lineage. "We Are Family." We are the offsprings of a related, common group. And because of this common bond or bloodline, it is of no surprise that this uniqueness of ours unfolded into "a coming together again" to reunite on a happy occasion "after separation" into what has been named the Fleming-Malone Family Reunion.

As a descendant of either the Fleming bloodline, the Malone bloodline, or of both Fleming and Malone ancestry, "We Are Family" united by blood, by love, by association, by matrimony, by compassion, by concern, by care, and through friendship.

By circumstances, situation, or condition, "We Are Family" and will continue to be throughout our physical life. And when our appointed time has been exhausted, I pray we will be united again, one day as a spiritual family with our Heavenly Father.

I hope each of you will remember this day with fond memories and pass these and other collections of family treasures to your loved ones. I hope also that this family reunion, although our first, I pray that it will not be our last.

After we have left this July 7 Sunday morning service, and meet at the festivity later today, and as the day draws to a close and you travel back to your homes, I hope you will remember this day and these events, in years to come, with fond memories of a *happy* family reunion.

I welcome you and salute each of you. May God continue to bless each of us in a unique way according to our need.

Source of definitions: Webster's New World Dictionary.

Reverend Vernon V. Malone delivered the "Family" message. In memory of deceased loved ones and to mark the occasion, we planted shrubbery on the church lawn.

Later, a catered luncheon was held at the Somerville Civic Center where the family became acquainted with each other — many for the first time — swapped family stories, took snapshots, and shared family albums.

We decided to price the day's activities by event, with the purchases from the specially designed T-shirts defraying the expense of the church programs, plaques, and certificates. The cost of the luncheon paid for itself and helped to offset the cost of the continental breakfast. The unanticipated expenditures were absorbed by the planners.

When the planners of the Edmondson-Lillard Family Reunion

began planning their slate of events, their ideas formed and resulted in two days of scheduled activities (see Appendix D).

July 27, 1986
Meeting held at the home of Sarah Johnson.
The meeting was called to order by the chairperson.
The program committee gave its report. It was submitted in writing for approval by the membership. The approved activities follow:

Friday — Wine and Cheese Social — Home of Victoria Overton
6 to 9 p.m.
Saturday — Picnic — site to be selected
1 p.m. to 4 p.m.
Food to be catered
Dance/Fashion Show — site to be selected
7 p.m.-until
Music provided by James Johnson

A questionnaire will be sent to all family members requesting fashion and talent participants.

The Leath-Kage (see Appendix C) planners settled on a two-day reunion beginning with hospitality night, followed by a picnic the next day and ending with a talent show and dance. While the Ma Jane Gardner family chose a banquet style to welcome guests and make presentations of awards, the Leath-Kage made their presentations during Hospitality Night.

While you may have already considered several ideas to use, here are some additional suggestions to select from: menus, games, souvenirs, events and activities to add to your list of possibilities.

Some Suggested Activities

Picnic Menu (catered)
(Based on 250 people attending)
Barbecue Sliced Beef
Barbecue Chicken

Potato Salad
Baked Beans
Sliced Bread
Assorted desserts — cakes, pies, and cookies
Beverage — tea, lemonade, fruit drinks
Relishes — Assortment
Fresh Fruit — in season

Some families might wish to prepare their own food. And if you decide you'd prefer doing this rather than having it catered, that's fine. But remember most of the preparation will fall to the hosting families because those traveling from a distance cannot bring certain foods with them.

Backyard Cookout
Hot Dogs
Hamburgers
Sandwiches
Potato Chips
Relishes — Assortment
Fresh Fruit — in season
Beverages — tea, lemonade, fruit drinks

If you should decide on a backyard-type family picnic, some other items to add to the above food list include:

1. paper plates and cups
2. plastic knives, forks, spoons and serving utensils, including tongs
3. paper napkins
4. large pot or grill for heating weiners
5. available grill for cooking hamburgers and keeping buns warm
6. aluminum foil
7. charcoal and kindling, plus matches and starter fluid
8. garbage bags to dispose of waste
9. pot holders or gloves
10. ice chest
11. packing boxes

Dinner Banquet Menus

Menu I
Waldorf Salad
Tossed Salad with Dressing
Fried Chicken
Sliced Roast Beef
Baked Ham
Augratin Potatoes
Green Beans Almondine
Hot, Spiced Apple Slices
Rolls and butter
Assorted Desserts
Coffee, Tea, and Milk

Menu II
Tossed Salad with Dressing
Cajun or Blackened Fish
Baked Ham
Sliced Roast Beef
Wild Rice
Broccoli with Cheese Sauce
Rolls and Butter
Assorted Desserts
Coffee, Tea, and Milk

Fun Activities

Picnic
Backyard Cookout
Hiking
Skiing
Roller or Ice Skating

Swap & Talent Shop Time
Cocktail Hour
Hospitality Hour
Party/Formal Dance

Swap and Talent Show

An added touch to a traditional kind of family reunion is the Swap and Talent Shop. It is an ideal time to display handicrafts that members of the family are willing to swap, sell, or just show.

Here's a list of some of what you could display at a Swap and Talent Show. You probably have other ideas you could add to this list:

drawings, paintings	coin collections
poetry	stamp collections
handmade clothing	jewelry
stitchery — knitting	book collections
leather goods	floral arrangements
Indian crafts	pottery
family portraits	quilts

Games

potato race	dominoes
three-legged race	cards
baseball or softball	tug-o-war
horseshoes	frisbee
checkers	racing
volleyball	etc.

Souvenirs

Address book imprinted with _____ Family Reunion (date)
Tea towel calendar
T-shirts
Cassette tape of formal affair
Video movie
Copy of newspaper on the date of reunion
Pot holders (for women)
Key rings
Bumper stickers or appropriate decals
Tourist information

Plus More Things to Do

1. Decorate the host home with a WELCOME sign or _____ Family Reunion sign in the family theme colors
2. Balloons on the mail box are sure to warm up guests
3. Decorate the front door
4. Or use all of these. The warmer, the happier the kick-off to a reunion

Schedule of Events

FRIDAY, JULY 17:
(Adults)
Get Acquainted Party
7 p.m.-until
Dress: casual
(Youth, 13 to 18 years old)
Teen Party
7 p.m. until 12 p.m.
Dress: casual (shirts and shoes required)
(Infants and Children to 12 years)
Refreshments and Games

Shuttle and Van Services pick up from hotel parking lot at 6:30 p.m. and return after festivities

SATURDAY, JULY 18:
Family Picnic
12 noon-4 p.m.
Dress: sports attire

Fashion-Talent Show and Dinner Party
6 p.m.-midnight
(Cocktails at 6 p.m.)
Dress: evening/semi-formal

SUNDAY, JULY 19:
Memorial Service
Time: TBA
Dress: appropriate

The Last Round Up
Bon Voyage Party — hotel ballroom
1 p.m. until departure

CHAPTER 4

ESTABLISHING A WORKING BUDGET

The next step is to create a budget. This should be done by itemizing each day's events. How much must each family member pay to defray the cost of the reunion?

Cost will be one of the key questions asked and you must be prepared to give the facts. You can be sure Aunt Clara, whose total income is derived from her retirement and Social Security, will want to know--maybe even in detail--as others probably will also. So be cost-conscious in setting the amount to be borne by each person or family.

Cost Sharing Per Person/Family

Be specific regarding how the money will be used. For example, if you say the cost to attend all functions is a one-time fee of $25 per person or $50 per family of four, then specify precisely what an individual or family will get for their money. Here are two suggested ways to explain this (more detail later in the chapter):

The cost to attend is $25 per person/$12.50 per child 12 years and under, which includes your pass to the Hospitality Hour, Banquet, and Picnic.

Each adult is being asked to pay $25 and each child 12 years and under $12.50 to defray all costs. This admits you to the fashion awards program, picnic, and contribution to Mount Calvary Baptist Church from the Family Reunion Fund.

Right away you have given some, if not all, details of how the money will be spent. Without this explanation, I can assure you there will be such questions as: "What are they going to do with all that money?" Some groundwork will need to be done as soon as possible after you have gained the interest of a few who have made known their intention to come. It may even be necessary to have some ideas about cost factors before committees begin their work, because this information should go out to the family in the first or at least by the second mailing you send.

The dollar amount you finally settle on should not be set so tightly that you have not left some leeway to cover items not already factored into the budget. A good example is if the caterer initially settled on cannot prepare the kind of dessert you want at the price first quoted. You then find another caterer who can do it for you but the price is higher. Members of the family will not look favorably upon the planners if three months before the reunion you write asking for an additional $10 to cover something you did not know about earlier.

Request that family members pay at least one half of the agreed amount within 30 days from the receipt of the letter, with the other half due 90 days before the reunion. This will assure working capital and at the same time give some idea about how many people to expect.

The sample budget on pages 35-36 is based on 250 people attending. Although this is a hypothetical budget which can be decreased or increased depending on your particular family, it's possible that, even though you come from a relatively small family, by the time you add in-laws and perhaps close family friends, the number can easily come close to this planning figure.

Most caterers, if you should decide to use one, are accustomed to preparing large buffets and banquets and usually prepare for 5-10 settings above the quoted attendance number. That way they have allowed for a slightly marginal increase. Of course, there is the possibility of having to pay for no-shows; this is unavoidable, whether planning for 10 people or 100 people.

Keep in mind when setting participant fees that some kind of travel will be necessary for some members of the family. Once you have some idea of the distances they must travel to get to the reunion, check on travel cost by bus, plane, train, or automobile. Take the farthest distance and add up the total cost in out-of-pocket money a person will possibly need to spend in order to attend (refer to Appendices for assistance). The expense involved could be a deciding factor. After you've gotten this information, it may be necessary to trim down your activities so as not to price anyone out of attending by setting the rate too high.

There are ways to be frugal and still have a good time. Just as in our everyday lives, there are some people who have less disposable income than others, and some who have more. This also applies to certain branches of one's family. Try not to create undue hardship on anyone. A family reunion is intended as a fun time. You want to be reasonable with your planning activities and be keen-minded to the cost of travel expenses. Again, this is another reason to set the date as far in advance as possible. Therefore, one year before is not an unreasonable time to notify everyone of the plans to coordinate a family reunion.

A Sample Family Reunion Budget

Based on 250 attendees--200 adults @ $50 each and 50 children @ $25 each child over 12 for a total working budget of **$11,250**

Day I -- Banquet

Based on $25 per adult and $12.50 each child 12 years and under:

$ 5,625

Day II -- Family Picnic

Catered — at $6 per adult and $3.50 per child 12 years and under — include food, drinks, ice, paper cups and plates, plastic knives, forks, spoons, paper napkins, tablecloths, etc.

$ 1,275

Day III -- Memorial Service (for deceased loved ones)

Individual contribution and/or _____ Family Reunion Fund	**0 - $250**
Bon Voyage Reception	**$ 750**

Other Expenditures:

Plaques: 8x10, 5x7	**$ 200**
Certificates (250)	**$ 25**
Printing; copying	**$ 200**
T-shirts and sun visors or baseball caps	**$ 1,125**
Souvenirs	**$ 200**
Newspaper: 200x35 cents	**$ 70**
Stationery and postage	**$ 200**
Musicians	**$ 300**
Miscellaneous (waiters, bartenders, helpers, rentals)	**$ 250**
TOTAL	**$10,220 — $10,470**

Contingency Funds

You may be tempted to price a per-person cost individually per day's event, because some people may be able to attend only a certain portion, if the reunion lasts for more than one day. As simple as it might seem on the surface to do this, it is not the best way. There are up-front expenses that you may not be able to build in using this method. The people who plan the event should not end up "holding the bag" because of the unexpected, even though you planned very carefully.

Here's one scenario which comes to mind of an "unexpected": because of the temperature on the day of the picnic, the ice disappears one hour into the fun. What do you do? Search in your pocket for the money? Ask around the crowd in hopes you can gather up enough money from your relatives? Or do you go to the treasury for the funds? Can you imagine what the responses will be from the family if you were to ask for additional money on the day of the picnic?

The best way to prevent such an occurrence is to have funds in the treasury, of course. Then to run out of ice or cups or drinks would only be an inconvenience and not the hassle it could turn out to be without contingency monies available just for such a possibility.

The above example may seem unlikely, but in fact it is thoroughly possible. But if to have or not to have a reunion at all hinges on taxing relatives a flat $10, $20, or $30 — as opposed to a fee per activity — then the fee per activity can work; but not without many disadvantages and major recordkeeping. As mentioned earlier, one set fee could get a person into all events. There would be no hidden costs popping out of the woodwork. Relatives would get all amenities without worrying about additional costs. They could also plan their out-of-pocket expenses better.

On the other hand, in the fee-for-event method, specific people would need to be available to accept money throughout the reunion for relatives who decide at the last minute they want to purchase a T-shirt or buy tickets to the banquet or the picnic. The planners would not have a chance to enjoy themselves, which would be unfair since they are the ones who have already spent months behind the scene getting everything ready. What a shame it would also be if they did not have the same chance to mingle and mix along with other family members.

The sample form on page 39 can be used with some modifications for unit pricing items rather than a total cost for all events. This same form as shown can also be used for collecting order information.

How To Handle Excess Funds

Finally, decide how excess funds will be handled. Will the hosting planners maintain the bank account until the next reunion planners are named? Set up a _____ Family Scholarship Fund, in the name of the person who initiated the first reunion or perhaps dedicate it to the oldest living descendant. Setting up an educational fund with leftover monies is a great way to provide financial assistance to a deserving young person of the family. Investing in another person's education is a worthwhile way a family can give something of value to its younger generation.

Money used in this way supports an often needful and worthy cause, and, at the same time, serves to draw the family even closer together. Another idea might be to donate the money in the name of the designated hosting family's church, or to a favorite charity. Just be sure you get family consensus on the use of any leftover funds.

MY NAME AND ADDRESS ARE LISTED BELOW TO MAIL T-SHIRT ORDER:

NAME _____

ADDRESS _____

CITY _____ STATE _____ ZIP _____

TELEPHONE (   ) _____

DATE CHECK METHOD OF PAYMENT: _____ MONEY ORDER ENCLOSED
_____ CHECK
(SORRY, NO C.O.D.)

_____

QUANTITY	DESCRIPTION: SPECIAL INSTRUCTIONS, IF ANY	ADULTS	S I Z E	YOUTH	S I Z E	TOTAL PRICE

RETURN ORDER REQUEST TO:

ORDER TOTAL _____

TOTAL ENCLOSED _____

CHAPTER 5

SENDING ANNOUNCEMENTS

Now is the time to send an announcement or bulletin to family members. Give the specifics but be sure also to pepper your announcement with plenty of enthusiasm, with a pinch of what you envision the reunion to create. State the date or dates and location of the family reunion. All of this can very well be put in the form of a letter. However, be sure to solicit local family helpers as you deem necessary to get the job done. Whether you choose a more creative form to make the announcement or use the traditional letter, make sure it is appealing. Whet their appetite and spur their interest.

Beginning on page 44 you will find several samples of announcements, forms, and helpful tips to spark interest.

Include everything you have decided thus far. You can be brief and concise, and still include enough information to make those receiving it want to know more — this should be the name of the game. Include one or two additional copies to be passed on to those you were unable to contact personally.

It is a good idea to keep copies and an index file of contacts. Include a brief form for individuals to return expressing their interest in attending and if they wish to participate in certain activities. Ask also for addresses of other relatives so you may contact them directly in subsequent mailings as plans develop. Don't flood their mail boxes with letters every week. There is such a thing as overkill. Besides, postage can be expensive. But do communicate often enough to keep enthusiasm high. Generate their interest. The heightened interest could very well mean a lot of volunteers for committee work. Rather than a letter, post cards can do the same thing for you — generate interest and enthusiasm. The post card is also a less expensive way of keeping everyone informed in between explanatory or detailed correspondence.

The Pajama Game
(Hotel and Housing Accommodations)

Arrangements for housing may also be a part of your announcement letter or bulletin.

The committee or coordinator on housing will take care of selecting hotel accommodations or securing from local relatives rooms to put up travelers for the period of the reunion. You can provide relatives with a select list of hotels in the city and let them be responsible for their own reservations, which is probably the best avenue to take. That way it is less likely that there will be mistakes. Hotel personnel are trained for this kind of work and can usually do a better job as well. Also, you reduce your mailings because hotels are equipped to send confirmations direct. Two housing forms are on page 49 to assist you in acquiring rooming for out-of-town relatives with the in-town hosting planners.

Tips for Putting Up or Bedding Down Relatives

As the core planners, you especially want to show hospitality at its finest without overburdening yourself so that you won't have energy left to enjoy the reunion. Your home is not a hotel, so relatives should not expect room service. If you plan well, guests can be comfortable and relaxed and enjoy themselves at the same time while being a guest in your home.

Agree to house only the number you can adequately provide for. That means being well-stocked with the usual amenities:

Food:

Stock the fridge with food for the meals that will not be provided during the reunion activities.

Prepare ahead of time and freeze. Plenty of fresh fruit and beverages.

Bedding:

Cots and sleeping bags
Crib and playpen for infant

Linens:

Sheets
Pillows and pillow cases

Toiletries:

Soap
Toothpaste
Shaving cream
Deodorant, etc.

Towels:

Wash cloths
Bath towels
Hand towels

Miscellaneous

Assorted toys and games to entertain children.

The following pages of letters and sample forms will give you a clearer idea of how other families have handled sending notices.

Edmondson/Lillard
Family Reunion

July 17, 18, 19, 1987   *Nashville, Tenn.*

Dear Family Member,

Things are really happening in Nashville. The plans are shaping up nicely. We hope to see each and every one of you on July 17, 18, 19.

As you can see, we have our letterhead. This was designed by one of your own, Victor Hoggett, son of Sarah Johnson.

We are planning to make this a very memorable occasion beginning with Friday night and extending straight through Sunday afternoon. So plan to stay the entire weekend. There will be a social time on Friday, picnic on Saturday afternoon, dance/talent/fashion show on Saturday night, and church service on Sunday morning.

Some of you have sent your $10 initial fee. Thank you for being so prompt. The money is needed for planning and communications to let you know how we are progressing. We still need to hear from some of you. We want this to be the best reunion ever. Send your money as soon as possible. The next communication will have a list of the money received.

Remember the dates and plan to be here in Nashville on July 17, 18, and 19.

WE WANT TO SEE YOU!

Emma Osborne, Chairperson
The Nashville Group

Pat Allen, Secretary
The Nashville Group

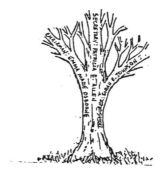

Dear Family Members:

There's excitement in the air, feelings of anxiousness, and feelings of caring and love, why? The celebration of the MA JANE GARDNER FAMILY REUNION activities scheduled for June 21 and 22 is just around the corner. My hearing about the excitement and the planning makes me happy also, because it is your participation that is going to make our reunion a gala affair.

I know we have a deadline of May 31 for our Banquet ticket money, but you can start now sending in payments so as not to make it so hard for you — we don't mind the extra bookkeeping. Also by sending in your monies as early as possible, this will enable me to communicate with the hotel in a more positive manner about your attendance to the Banquet. Jim and I know we can depend on you to get your Banquet registration money in to us.

The Program Committee has met and the Reunion acitivities were approved by our Reunion Committee. The Program Committee has laid out an excellent program that we think will be enjoyable and one that will be remembered for years to come. The Program Committee informs you of the following:

Our Reunion theme is "We Are the Children."

Our Family Reunion colors are red and white, and we are hoping everyone will wear something red and white at the picnic on Saturday.

Please familiarize your family with the new song entitled "We Are the World" for the night of the Banquet Program.

Nashville and surrounding family members, our Housing Committee chairpersons need to hear from you about available beds for our out-of-town members (see enclosed Housing Form).

Out-of-town family members, please contact the Housing Committee as to your needs for sleeping space by Sunday, June 16. Accommodations will be for Friday, June 21 through Sunday, June 23 only. With prior planning you will know with whom and where you will be staying (see enclosed Housing Form).

And for you family members who will really have vacationing fever, enclosed is a list of hotels in Nashville with their rates, locations and phone numbers. You are to arrange your own accommodations.

Nashville family members, I hope you're talking with your immediate family members about the picnic food. Our out-of-town family members are making plans in a big way to come, so let us be ready with plenty of good Southern food to share with them.

Our Program Committee would like to know if there are any musicians, soloist or group singers in the family. If so, please contact me or Pat quickly. And if you would like to participate on the program, contact Pat and she will work something out.

On Saturday, June 22, we will kick off our Family Picnic with a Family Meeting which will be held from 10 a.m. to 11 a.m. It is so important that you attend and be on time, for we must make some immediate decisions for our Reunion next year.

Immediately after the Family Meeting, there will be a time for sharing family photo albums — so bring an album and share with everyone some family roots. Also, there will be games and prizes for all to share in.

The Banquet will be held at the Downtown Sheraton Hotel, 920 Broadway, which is located across the street from Nashville's Main Post Office. For your information, the Hotel phone number is area code 615/244-0150. Traveling on the interstate, you exit I-40 at the Broadway or Demonbreun exit.

The picnic will be held at Cedar Hills Community Park, area 12. The park is located on Old Hickory Boulevard. Traveling on the Interstate you exit I-65N at the Madison/Old Hickory exit.

Let's continue to remain excited and encourage everyone, family and friends, to attend the historical event. If you have questions, ideas, criticisms, concerns, etc., please don't hesitate to let the Reunion Committee hear about them.

I hope I have not forgotten anything, so be certain to keep this letter and refer to it as this will be the last written communication the Committee will send you. So please, get your Banquet money in to Jim or me, contact the Housing Committee, Shirlithia or Alice, and make your plans to attend the Reunion activities — we feel that it will be an event you will always remember and cherish.

Sincerely,
Linda Crook Williams
Reunion Planning Committee

May 20, 1985

Dear Family Member:

No doubt by now you've heard from Debra about our FAMILY REUNION: "WE ARE FAMILY" on July 7.

I hope you and your family are planning to be there. While Debra is planning the activities for the family brunch at 9 a.m. and luncheon at 2 p.m., I am coordinating and writing the "Commemoration Ceremony" (In Remembrance of Loved Ones) on Sunday, July 7 to be held at the Mount Calvary Baptist Church beginning at 11 a.m.

Our own Reverend Vernon V. Malone will minister the sermon, "Family." I am seeking your participation in order for this to be a time of gratitude and thanksgiving and an event to remember for many years. But I need your talents for the program to be a success. I need people who are willing to sing in the choir, or do a solo, read a poem, or say a prayer, make the presentations, or participate in the candlelight tribute for deceased family members. If you are willing to do any of these things, please indicate on the enclosed form and return to me by June 15.

Also I am planning a Commemorative Souvenir Booklet in which I would like to include the history of each member's "Family Tree" (cost to be decided later). If you wish to have your family tree included in this keepsake, please return the enclosed form, along with a photograph of yourself (size should be at least 5x7). Snapshots will not print well. This information is also needed by June 15. The souvenir book will be a professionally printed keepsake that you can pass on to successive generations of our kinfolk. Please cooperate. Let's leave something tangible of ourselves for our children and children's children.

Finally, one last request. Please send me a list of your loved ones you wish to pay tribute to during the memorial service.

I think this is going to be a memorable occasion, and I look forward to seeing you on July 7.

BE THERE! WE GUARANTEE YOU'LL HAVE A WONDERFUL TIME.

With warm affection,

Emma J. Wisdom

WANTED

ALL BRANCHES OF THE

FAMILY TREE

LAST SEEN:

Short time ago; not so long ago; more than two years ago

VITAL STATISTICS:

Known to be loved

Comes from a good tree branch

Nurtured from a tiny twig

May be a tiny twig or a strong branch

ALERT:

If you know the whereabouts or have seen any member of this family tree in your vicinity, GET ADDRESS AND TELEPHONE NUMBER — CONTACT US IMMEDIATELY

Housing Committee
Available Beds

I, _____ will be able to sleep _____ people for our Reunion. I have sleeping arrangements for:

Check Your Desire

____ Adults ____ Entire Family ____Teenagers ____ Does Not Matter

Other Restrictions: _____

Instructions

For our records, please indicate your address and phone number

Your Name _____

Street _____

City _____ State _____ Zip _____

Phone _____

Please return this form to Shirlithia or Alice or call us no later than June 15.

Housing Committee
Housing Needs

I, _____ will need _____ sleeping spaces. Instructions: Please give the names and ages of each person in your family needing sleeping space _____

_____

_____

Please give your address and phone below:

Your Name _____

Street _____

City _____ State _____ Zip _____

Mail this form to:

_____

Enclose an Acceptance Form to make it easier for individuals to volunteer their services. From this data you will be able to get a good idea of the number planning to attend.

Acceptance Form

Name _____

Street _____

City _____ State _____ Zip _____

Telephone (   ) _____

I plan to attend the Family Reunion activities. I am enclosing $30 each for _____ adult reservations and $25 each for _____ 12 year old and under reservations. For the record, I am a descendant of _____. I intend to bring the following friend(s) and my check covers the appropriate cost:

ADULT	CHILD
1. _____	1. _____
2. _____	2. _____
3. _____	3. _____

Please list the name(s) above. Submit payment by: Check or Money Order. Return form along with check or money order to:

Name _____

Street _____

City _____ State _____ Zip _____

Fashion/Talent Show Form

We have planned a Fashion-Talent Show for the evening of Saturday, July 18, 1987. In order for this event to occur we need you as a volunteer. Please fill out the questionnaire below.

Name _____

Street _____

City _____ State _____ Zip _____

Telephone (   ) _____

1. I would like to participate in the Fashion Show _____ Yes _____ No
2. I will be modeling the following: (Formal, Casual, Swim Wear)

_____

3. I would like to participate in the Talent Show _____ Yes _____ No
4. I will entertain by: _____
5. Length of performance: _____ minutes
6. Number in group: _____

NOTE: If you're in the fashion show you must bring your own apparel. Equipment other than microphone and stereo must be supplied by performer.

Reservation Form

I am interested in obtaining a copy of the Commemorative Souvenir Booklet as a keepsake of the _____ Family Tree. I understand the cost of this historical booklet will be determined by the printing cost (estimate $8 — $10).

Please reserve _____ copy(ies) for me.

Name _____

Street _____

City _____ State _____ Zip _____

Telephone (____) _____

Return Form to: _____

_____

_____

General Information

An added touch when traveling is to have some information about the place you're about to visit. That is one reason tourism is now big business in major cities. They print lots of facts to attract travelers which are then advertised and distributed throughout the country.

Contact your local office on tourism and request a number of brochures to mail to relatives. (Refer to the Appendices for local and out-of-state addresses and telephone numbers.) Any free time between family activities can be ON YOUR OWN time spent perhaps touring the city. Most cities have historical and other attractive points of interest they can visit for a pleasant and enjoyable time. If you're unable to get this information in your own city, create your own fact sheet of information tips and use it as a stuffer in one of your last mailings shortly before the date of the reunion. Some information you might wish to include as a bulletin:

BULLETIN

*** *NASHVILLE CLIMATE.* Warm and sunny to hot and humid during summer months. Temperature ranges from 72 to 94 degrees.

*** GET ACQUAINTED RECEPTION. *ATTIRE*: A come-as-you-are affair for early evening arrivals.

*** PICNIC. *ATTIRE*: Casual with comfortable shoes.

*** BANQUET. *ATTIRE*: After five attire for women and dress suit for men.

*** BON VOYAGE (Departure Party). *ATTIRE*: Traveling home attire.

FOUR EXTRAS TO MAKE
A FAMILY REUNION SPECIAL

1. Music

Decide on type of music suitable for the occasion.

Select each tune you wish played.

Go over details with the musicians of special music to be played at specific points in the program.

Instruct musicians to provide a variety of tunes suitable to the young set as well as for the older members of the family. Have the band start with popular tunes from the 20's and play right through to the present.

2. Photographs and Videotapes

The next closest thing to the memories you'll have long after the reunion is over is to capture the entire event on snapshots and videotapes. You can leaf through your album or view a videotape months and years later. These mementos can serve as a way of reliving and renewing the glow almost exactly to the extent that you felt on that day.

But investigate thoroughly photographers you are interested in hiring. Review their portfolio to see the quality of their work.

3. Snapshots

Send an Update Card to each relative asking for information about children born since the last family reunion to be returned along with a recent snapshot. Create a biographical sketch. Place the snapshot in the center top of a standard 8 1/2 x 11 sheet of paper. Type the bio below. Use construction paper to create a frame. Display in a conspicuous place during the reunion activities.

Biographical Data Sheet
(Information to Request)

Name _____ Birth Date _____

Nickname_____ Place of Birth_____

Vital Statistics: Height _____ Weight _____

Eye Color _____ Hair Color _____ Other Distinguish-
ing Features _____

Mother's Maiden Name _____ Nickname _____

Father's Name _____ Nickname _____

Present Address _____

Telephone Number (   ) _____

Return Photo Along With Form To: _____

---

4. Mayor's Proclamation

At the time that you prepare your press release, send a similar letter using the information from your release to the mayor of your city.
One family was able to get a beautiful suitable-for-framing Mayor's
Proclamation honoring their family on the day of the reunion presented
by a representative from the Mayor's office. Shortly following the
reunion, you might have laminated miniature copies made to send to
participants in the form of a key ring similar to the small diplomas given
to a school's graduates.

Writing the Press Release

Your publicity and communications committee is important for
promoting the reunion. Write up a press release to send to the local
newspapers where the reunion will be held and other cities where there
are clusters of relatives. Contact the newspapers in your city in order
to be certain as to whom you should address your correspondence.
Usually it's the society or lifestyles editor or events reporter. It may take

one or two calls, or several, before you reach the right person. However, an announcement in the city newspaper means free publicity for a community event in your area.

Most newspapers usually carry human interest stories. Unusual tidbits picked up from press releases can sometimes lead to an extended article. Honoring someone who is 90 years old, returning to his or her childhood home for the first time in 30, 40, 50, or perhaps 60 years would make for a good human interest story. Will a sister or brother be reunited after separation by adoption years ago? If you have some unusual facts about a relative, be sure to include a few chosen words to explain. Enclose photos of older members of the family.

These are only a few community interest stories which could cause more than a brief announcement in your local newspaper. Editors decide to do stories for many different reasons. They have been known to send a photographer to take pictures. You never know! So it certainly will not hurt to send a press release. You could get miles out of a concise and informative writeup. Or you could end up with a piece just as you sent it,but any way it turns out, you have lost nothing. You can gain much, however.

The planners of the Ma Jane Gardner Family reunion's press release on page 56 illustrates in its original form what you might include for your own family's release to your local newspapers.

Criteria for Writing a Press Release

Be creative. You need not be a great writer. Just state the facts of WHO, WHAT, WHEN, WHERE. Your news release should be sent about six weeks before. Then follow up two weeks before the activities begin. Newspapers are often pressed for space, but sometimes they will be only too pleased to have interesting copy.

Be prepared: it is likely that your release will be edited. Therefore, state the most important points first; the second most important information; the third; and so on. That way if the piece must be cut or edited because of inadequate space, your most important data will be kept. Finally, your finished copy should be about 500 words but no more than 750 typed, double spaced on white quality paper.

In the upper left hand corner of the page indicate contact person and telephone number and to the right RELEASE DATE. Negotiate with the editor to run the press release on the day of the reunion. Order enough copies for every adult attending the reunion as a souvenir. Take a marking pen and write across the top of the newspaper in bold letter-ing _____Family Reunion. What a thoughtful, added attraction this could be!

Send a copy of your release to selected community radio and television stations as well. Although your primary source for spreading the word may be newspapers, don't overlook these two additional media sources. Both may be willing to broadcast the event in their area. If you've had difficulty reaching family members, radio and television can also be great potential sources of help in this area.

Contact Person: Linda Williams   **For Release:** June 21
Telephone: (609) 999-2222

NEWS RELEASE

One-hundred twenty-five (125) family members focusing on seven (7) generations of the MA JANE GARDNER FAMILY REUNION will convene on Friday and Saturday, June 21-22, 1985 in Nashville, Tennessee.

The activities will include a Banquet on Friday, June 21, which is being held at the Nashville Downtown Sheraton Hotel. While enjoying a buffet dinner, special recognitions will be given to Joe Maclin, the oldest living descendant, and Millie Batey McGee, the descendant who has been most fruitful in the continuation of the family lineage. Also the program will consist of a fashion show featuring family members.

For the occasion, the Family has chosen the theme, "We Are the Children," and has adopted as its Family Song the popular lyrics, "We Are the Children of the World."

On Saturday, June 22, the Family Picnic will be held at the Cedar Hills Community Park on Old Hickory Boulevard. The family colors are red and white and everyone will be wearing specially designed T-shirts in celebration of the occasion.

Members of the family are making plans to attend traveling from New York, Indiana, Michigan, Kentucky, Texas, and Alabama, to join Tennessee family members as a part of the reunion gathering.

CHAPTER 6

REVIEWING PLANNED ACTIVITIES

P roblems will arise and decisions will need to be made, but if you planned well, you will be able to handle any situation. In this case, committees can be worth their weight in gold. If they do their work well, committees will prevent situations from ballooning beyond the limits of control.

Having a well-honed team of family workers and defining responsibilities give the added assurance that things will get done properly. One committee can select caterers and plan menus; another can plan for decoration, while another may be expected to handle games and prizes at the picnic. Whatever your team decides should be within some particular area of responsibility. Sharing responsibilities among a few willing workers is usually enough inspiration for most of us to weather almost any storm to bring about a successful outcome.

What has been accomplished with other families you, too, can achieve within your family unit. Reunion planning should be approached just as you would tackle a business project. Take the bigger tasks, break each into small segments, and you should have no problem in bringing about a great family reunion, one that will hold fond memories for many years.

If you recall, it was recommended earlier that planners start working at least twelve months before the date of the occasion and no less than a six month lead time period. It's not that these kinds of events are complex or difficult. There are, however, many and varied tasks to be done, as has been pointed out throughout these pages. The number of days the reunion will go on also can determine how long it will take to finalize the plans. But what other families have done to keep ancestral ties close and to continue or to start a family tradition, you, too, can pull off.

Now the time draws nigh. It's only a few hours until "V" day when participants will begin to arrive. Excitement is high. But, of course, you're a little anxious to know if family members will be pleased and if everything will go off well. Just remind yourself that you've planned well, but to ease your mind look over your final checklist to review the scheduled plan of events for any possible loopholes.

Final Checklist

____1. Has all the registration money been received?

____2. Have souvenirs been accounted for?

____3. Will there be enough of everything?

____4. Has a photographer been hired?

____5. Do you have enough money in the bank account to pay all the bills?

____6. Is everything scheduled to arrive on time? What are the delays? Can they be avoided?

____7. Are the certificates, awards, and plaques ready?

____8. Have equipment and stage props been rented or borrowed for the fashion-talent show?

____9. Has the final count been given to the hotel for the banquet and to the caterers for the picnic?

____10. Have servers and helpers been hired?

____11. Who will contact the newspaper again regarding the press release? Have copies of the newspaper for participants been ordered?

____12. Are there a sufficient number of games and prizes to entertain the children?

____13. Decoration ready? Welcome sign?

____14. Is there adequate housing? Is someone available to answer housing questions? Do you have enough cots, sleeping bags, etc. for those rooming with relatives?

___15. Are the treasurer and secretary prepared to handle the Registration Desk?

___16. Name plates and I.D. tags ready?

___17. Do you have adequate refreshments for the Get Acquainted or Bon Voyage parties?

___18. Transportation and drivers available for carrying guests to and from events?

You have arrived! As the planners, you now become the Hosting Families. It will fall on your shoulders to make everything seem effortless.

From the moment the first guest arrives in your city, on your door step, or at the motel or hotel where reservations were made, the _____ Family Reunion has begun!

The kickoff event you have planned, which is usually a Hospitality Hour or a Get Acquainted Party, will set the tone for the remainder of your time together. Most people are usually forgiving if things go wrong after the First Impression has been made, but less so in the beginning when one's expectations are running high. In any event, I hope the suggestions and ideas found throughout these pages have built your confidence enough that you believe you can pull off a reunion for your family as many others have done.

Part III

After-Reunion Tasks

Anything conceivable and believable is achievable.

CHAPTER 7

SUMMING UP

No reunion is quite over even after the last guest has left. There are a few clean-up tasks the planners must complete.

Perhaps you've been paying your bills as you've gone along, which lessens the number you have to take care of after the reunion festivities are over. If no bills are left to pay, you will probably need to return rental and borrowed items, carry out the wishes of the family of what to do with any leftover funds in the bank account and, finally, send Thank You notes to participants and especially to your helpers.

Thank You Notes

The last task of the planning committee is to send the Thank You notes. Refer to your file index that you began developing from the beginning to get the names and addresses of all family members. Compare with the list used during registration or sign-in of guests on the day of the reunion.

Now combine the names and addresses into one for easy handling. Two messages that show what you might want to include in your notes follow:

Dear _____,

       We were delighted to have you join us during the celebration of the _____ Family Reunion on July 3, 4, and 5.

       As you recall, the family voted during the reunion to have another one again next year over the Fourth of July weekend. We hope you will be able to join us in Nashville. So mark your calendar and plan to be there. Don't forget.

       Again, from all of us here, thank you for helping to make our first _____ Family Reunion a great success.

       With fond memories,

Another Thank You note might read:

Dear _____,

       The _____ Family Reunion on July 3, 4, and 5 was a great success. Thanks for coming.

       Hope you and your family will be able to join us next year in Nashville.

       Again, our thanks for your participation. It seems we've started a family tradition.

       With fond memories,

Special Note

Generally, Thank You notes are handwritten, but because of the volume this may not be practical. With advances in the print medium, you'll probably be able to find a good printing company to produce Thank You notes in script for you at a modest cost. This will give them that personal touch look.

Memories

Now that you have completed your tasks as the primary planner and "spark" for a successful family reunion, sit back, kick off your shoes, put up your feet, and relish in what you've accomplished. Smell the roses! Enjoy all the fond memories you've created for yourself and a host of grateful relatives for...

EPILOGUE

The family is the foundation of society. Family means different things to different people. To some people it means mother and father, sisters and brothers; to some it means the central structure including aunts and uncles and grandparents; to others it could extend to cousins and in-laws; but in today's society it could even mean all of these variables plus step-father and step-mother, step-sisters and step-brothers, and the kin-folks from each of these families. Regardless of how few or how extensive, "family" means love in all its varying degrees.

Forty years ago, families lived in the same community or within a few miles of each other and family gatherings were common on holidays and weekends or for no special reason at all other than to be in the company of each other. No extensive or involved planning was necessary. The family would decide to spend the weekend or Sunday afternoon with their parents, at Aunt Lillie's or Uncle Stan's house, or some other close members of the family.

A telephone call or short note would make your intentions known. Mom and Dad piled food and children into the old jalopy and off you went. That was that. Nothing more was needed. And after dinner, stories were swapped while children played with brothers and sisters, cousins and nearby neighbors. At an appointed time before you wore out your welcome you all piled back into the old family car and headed home. The next holiday the visit might have been reciprocated. But it wasn't necessary to plan these trips months in advance.

With today's transient family lifestyles, this is not usually the case. Family members may live on distant shores — from East to West, North to South — and any combination or location in between or overseas. The once-a- year, well-planned family reunion has taken the place of the frequent weekend or holiday jaunts. The family reunion may be the only alternative many of us have who live away from their original hometown of seeing loved ones.

The advantage to the new kind of family gathering is that a family reunion brings all family members together at one time. Because you do not see them as often as you would like, this fact alone is even more reason for the high- spirited enthusiasm and excitement family reunions tend to create. You are more prone to cherish the precious time you have together than ever before.

So if you have selected working committees and chairpersons, developed a realistic budget, planned activities based on expected, available funds, had regular, productive meetings, there's every indication that your family reunion will be everything you want it to be. Good luck, happy reunion time. Planning a family reunion is great fun! And during the family reunion, don't forget to put out feelers for next year or the next year for coordinators. Get started early.

It is now time to put your ideas to work planning your family reunion. Don't forget to let me know if it turns out to be everything you had anticipated and planned.

And in the spirit of Alex Haley's invaluable work, remember: the family you reunion with today represents the roots of future generations; if we plant the seed today, nurture the roots, the tree will grow strong to face the world tomorrow.

Appendix A

FLEMING-MALONE FAMILY REUNION

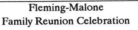

Fleming-Malone
Family Reunion Celebration

Sunday, July 7, 1985
11:00 a.m.
Reverend Vernon V. Malone, Minister
Emma Jackson Wisdom, Mistress of Ceremony
Mount Calvary Baptist Church
Somerville, Texas

Theme: "We Are Family"

Colors: Green & Gold

Programme

Enter to Worship *** Depart to Serve

The Prelude
Call to Worship
Congregational Hymn
Invocation
Congregational Hymn
Litany of Thanksgiving
Solo
Offeratory (Family Contribution)
Recognition of Guests
"The Occasion"
Memorial Tribute
Solo
Sermon: "Family"
Presentations
Acknowledgments
Benediction

Appendix B

MA JANE GARDNER FAMILY REUNION

Sheraton Hotel (Downtown)
Nashville, Tennessee
June 21, 1985
6:00 p.m.

Programme	*** Family Picnic ***
Patricia Crook — Mistress of Ceremony	
Presentation from Mayor's Office	Saturday, June 22, 1985
Welcome	Cedar Hills Community Park
Solo	Old Hickory Boulevard
Prayer	Nashville, Tennessee
"The Occasion"	
Solo	
Fashion Show	Planning Committee
Presentation of Awards	(May be listed if desired)
Announcements	
Musical Selection — "We Are the World"	Acknowledgments
Benediction	
	The 1985 MA JANE GARDNER
*** Buffet Dinner ***	FAMILY REUNION COMMITTEE
(menu may be listed if preferred)	extends a hearty and warm "thank you"
	for your participation.
Reunion Logo Design by Patricia Crook	
Family Theme: WE ARE THE CHILDREN	
Colors: Red and White	

Appendix C

LEATH-KAGE FAMILY REUNION

The Family

"Family is the oldest human institution. In many ways it is the most important. It is society's most basic unit."

In ancient Hebrew society the family was the basic unit. The family was a small government, the father as head being responsible to God, and the mother as the subordinate manager over the children in the household.

Individuals belong to two (2) primary families, the first as children and the second as parents. We are born into the first family and we establish the second one.

Family re-unions enable us to strengthen our bonds of love and to remain close-knit. Therefore, it is hopeful that the re-union of the Kage and Leath Klan will accomplish this end.

* Source: World Book Encyclopedia, 1973

*** Hospitality Night ***

Friday, August 1, 1986
7-9 p.m.
Two Rivers Mansion
Social Hour with music by Nelson Young
"The Occasion"
Welcome to "Out-of-Towners"
Presentation of Families
Memorial Observance

*** Picnic ***
Saturday, August 2, 1986
9 a.m. — 6 p.m.
Edwin Warner Park
Fun/Games/and Food!

*** Talent Show and Party ***
8 p.m. — 2 a.m.
Howard Johnson Motel
Arinetta Utley — Mistress of Ceremony

Programme

Solo
Impersonation
Solo
Lip Synching
Rapping
Solo
Trio
Duet
Finale

Music By: Nelson Young

Appendix D

EDMONDSON-LILLARD FAMILY REUNION

WE ARE FAMILY

EDMONDSON/LILLARD

HOLIDAY INN NORTH — TRINITY LANE
July 18, 1987
Time: 7:00 p.m. — 12:00 a.m.
Tracy Bunch
Mistress of Ceremony

---

7 p.m.   Cocktails
Fashion-Talent Show
8-10 p.m. PROGRAMME
        Welcome to Out-of-Town Family
           Members
        "The Occasion"
        Special Presentations
        Introduction of the:

           Tennessee Group
           Illinois Group
           Florida Group
           Texas Group
           Michigan Group
           California Group

LET THE FUN BEGIN!

For the next hour you will be entertained by
 family members with SONG, FASHION,
AND COMEDY ... ENJOY ... ENJOY

*** Dance ***

10 p.m. — 12 a.m.

Cut a Dance Step to Music From the
Past Right Up To Present-Day Popular Tunes

J A R O C K (a.k.a. James Johnson)
Disc Jockey

Organizers
(May be listed here, if desired)

Appendix E:
State and City Offices of Tourism
With Across-the-U.S.A. Reservations

Contact these state and city offices and request their vacation or trip planning kit. You will be able to get a good idea of the schedule of activities going on during the time you're planning to be in the area. Also, you might wish to schedule your reunion dates around these events. Calls to 800 numbers are toll-free; dial "1" then the number.

Bureau of Tourism and Travel   800-ALABAMA
532 S. Perry Street
Montgomery, AL 36104

Arizona Office of Tourism   (602) 255-3618
Suite 180
1480 E. Bethany Home Road
Phoenix, AZ 85014

Arkansas Department of Parks   800-482-8999
and Tourism   (Arkansas Residents)
1 Capital Mall   800-643-8383
Little Rock, AR 72201   (out of state)

California Office of Tourism   (916) 322-1397
Department of Commerce   800-862-2543
P. O. Box 9278   (out of state)
Van Nuys, CA 91409

Office of Tourism   (303) 592-5410
Colorado Tourism Board
1625 Broadway, Suite 1700
Denver, CO 80202

Delaware Tourism Office   800-441-8846
Delaware Development Office
99 Kings Highway
P. O. Box 1401
Dover, DE 19903

District of Columbia   (202) 789-7000
Washington Convention and
Visitors Association
1575 Eye Street, NW, Suite 250
Washington, DC 20005

Department of Commerce   (904) 487-1462
Visitors Inquiry
126 Van Buren Street
Tallahassee, FL 32399-2000

Tourist Division   (404) 656-3590
230 Peachtree Street
Suite 605
Atlanta, GA 30303

Hawaii Visitors Bureau   (808) 923-1811
2270 Kalakaua Avenue
Suite 801
Honolulu, HI 96815

Department of Commerce   (208) 334-2470
Statehouse, Room 108   (Idaho Residents)
Boise, ID 83720   800-635-7820
                                                    (out of state)

Illinois Department of Commerce   (217) 782-7139
and Community Affairs
Office of Tourism
620 East Adams Street
Springfield, IL 62701

Indiana Department of Commerce   (317) 232-8860
Tourism Development Division
1 North Capitol, Suite 700
Indianapolis, IN 46204-2288

Iowa Development Commission   (515) 281-3100
Visitors and Tourism
200 East Grand Avenue
Des Moines, IA 50309

Travel, Tourism, and Film   (913) 296-2009
Services Division
Department of Economic Development
400 West 8th Street, 5th Floor
Topeka, KS 66603

Department of Travel Development   800-255-TRIP
Capital Plaza Tower, 22nd Floor
Frankfort, KY 40601

Office of Tourism   800-334-8626
P. O. Box 94291
Baton Rouge, LA 70804-9291

Maine Publicity Bureau   (207) 289-2423
97 Wintrop Street
P. O. Box 2300
Hallowell, ME 04347-2300

Office of Tourist Development   (301) 974-3517
45 Calvert Street
Annapolis, MD 21401

Department of Food and Agriculture   (617) 727-3018
Bureau of Markets
100 Cambridge Street
Boston, MA 02202

Travel Bureau   (517) 373-1195
Department of Commerce   800-543-2YES
P. O. Box 30226
Lansing, MI 48909

Minnesota Office of Tourism   800-328-1461
375 Jackson Street, Suite 250
St. Paul, MN 55101

Division of Tourism   (601) 359-3414
Department of Economic Development
P. O. Box 849
Jackson, MS 39205-0849

Missouri Division of Tourism   (314) 751-4133
P. O. Box 1055
Jefferson City, MO 65102

Travel Promotion   800-548-3390
Department of Commerce
1424 9th Avenue
Helena, MT 59620

Nebraska Tourism   800-742-7595
P. O. Box 94666   (Nebraska Residents)
Lincoln, NE 68509   800-228-4307
                                                       (out of state)

Commission on Tourism   (702) 885-4322
Capitol Complex
Carson City, NV 89710

Office of Vacation Travel   (603) 271-2666
P. O. Box 856
Concord, NH 03301

Division of Travel and Tourism   (609) 292-2470
CN-826
Trenton, NJ 08625

Tourism and Travel Division   800-545-2040
1100 St. Francis Drive
Santa Fe, NM 87503

Division of Tourism   (518) 474-4116
1 Commerce Plaza
Albany, NY 12245

Travel and Tourism Division   800-VISIT NC
Department of Commerce
430 North Salisbury Street
Raleigh, NC 27611

North Dakota Tourism Promotion   (701) 224-2525
Liberty Memorial Building   (North Dakota Residents)
Bismarck, ND 58505   800-437-2077
                                           (out of state)

Ohio Office of Travel and Tourism   800-BUCKEYE
P. O. Box 1001
Columbus, OH 43266-0101

Oklahoma Tourism and Recreation   (405) 521-2409
Department
Literature Distribution Center
215 NE 28th Street
Oklahoma City, OK 73105

Oregon Economic Development Department   (503) 378-3451
Tourism Division   (Oregon Residents)
595 Cottage Street, NE   800-547-7842
Salem, OR 97310   (out of state)

Bureau of Travel Development   (717) 787-5453
453 Forum Building
Harrisburg, PA 17120

Department of Economic Development   (401) 277-2601
Tourism and Promotion Division   (Rhode Island Residents)
Tourist Division   800-556-2484
7 Jackson Walkway   (out of state)
Providence, RI 02903

South Carolina Division of Tourism   (803) 734-0122
Box 71
Columbia, SC 29202

South Dakota Division of Tourism   800-843-1930
Capital Lake Plaza
Pierre, SD 57501

Department of Tourist Development	(615) 741-2158
P. O. Box 23170	
Nashville, TN 37202	
Travel Information Services	(512) 463-8588
State Highway Department	
P. O. Box 5064	
Austin, TX 78701	
Utah Travel Council	(801) 533-5681
Council Hall, Capitol Hill	
Salt Lake City, UT 84114	
Agency of Development and	(802) 828-3236
Community Affairs	
Travel Division	
134 State Street	
Montpelier, VT 05602	
Virginia Division of Tourism	(804) 786-4484
202 North Ninth Street	
Suite 500	
Richmond, VA 23219	
Washington State Tourism	800-544-9274
General Administration Building	or 544-1800
AX-13	(206) 586-2088
Olympia, WA 98504	or 586-2108
Travel Development--GOECD	800-CALL WVA
1900 Washington Street, East	
Charleston, WV 25305	
Department of Development	(608) 266-2161
Division of Tourism	
Box 7606	
Madison, WI 53707	
Wyoming Travel Commission	800-CALL WYO
I-25 at College Drive	
Cheyenne, WY 82002-0660	

Appendix F:
Hotel and Motel Sources
With Across-the-U.S.A. Reservations

Best Western (International)	800-528-1234
Days Inn	800-525-2525
Doubletree Hotels	800-538-0444

Drury Inn	800-325-8300
Executive Inn	800-482-8480
Four Seasons Hotels Ltd.	800-332-3442
Hallmark Inns of America	800-251-3294
The Hermitage Hotel	800-251-1908
Hilton Hotels	800-445-8667
Holiday Inn	800-465-4329
Howard Johnson Lodges & Hotels	800-654-2000
Hyatt Regency	800-228-9000
La Quinta Inns	800-531-5900
Lexington Hotel Suites	800-527-1877
Lincoln Hotels	800-228-0808
Marriott Hotels and Resorts	800-228-9290
Park Suite Hotel	800-822-2323
Quality Inn (Individual)	800-228-5151
(Groups)	800-638-2657
Radisson Hotels	800-228-9822
Ramada Inn (Reservations)	800-272-6232
(Group Meetings)	800-288-3344
Red Roof Inn	800-848-7878
Ritz Carlton Hotels	800-241-3333
Sheraton Hotels Inns & Resorts	800-325-3535
Shoney's Inn	800-222-2222
Stouffer Hotels	800-468-3571
Travelodge Motel	800-255-3050
Vanderbilt Plaza Hotel	800-228-0808
Westin Hotels & Resorts	800-228-3000

Appendix G:
Transportation Sources
Airlines With Across-the-U.S.A. Reservations

Allegheny Commuter	800-428-4253
	800-428-4322
American Airlines	800-334-7400
Delta Airlines	800-638-7333
Florida Express	800-327-8538
Pan Am	800-221-1111
Trans World Airlines (TWA)	800-438-2929
United Airlines	800-538-2929

Ground Transportation
With Across-the-U.S.A. Reservations

American Trailways	800-527-1566
Greyhound	800-528-0447
Amtrak	800-USA-RAIL

Auto Travel Information

POCKET ROAD ATLAS

Includes maps of the 50 states, Canada, and Mexico, with information on how to find the distance between two cities. Cost: $1.95.

1988 RAND MCNALLY ROAD ATLAS

Covers U.S., Canada, and Mexico, with information on 18 national parks, 1988 Fall, Winter, Spring, and Summer Calendar of Events across the U.S.A. Plus over $100 worth of Travel Discount Coupons. Cost: $6.95

1988

JANUARY

S	M	T	W	T	F	S
					1	2
3	4	5	6	7	8	9
10	11	12	13	14	15	16
17	18	19	20	21	22	23
24	25	26	27	28	29	30
31						

FEBRUARY

S	M	T	W	T	F	S
	1	2	3	4	5	6
7	8	9	10	11	12	13
14	15	16	17	18	19	20
21	22	23	24	25	26	27
28	29					

MARCH

S	M	T	W	T	F	S
		1	2	3	4	5
6	7	8	9	10	11	12
13	14	15	16	17	18	19
20	21	22	23	24	25	26
27	28	29	30	31		

APRIL

S	M	T	W	T	F	S
					1	2
3	4	5	6	7	8	9
10	11	12	13	14	15	16
17	18	19	20	21	22	23
24	25	26	27	28	29	30

MAY

S	M	T	W	T	F	S
1	2	3	4	5	6	7
8	9	10	11	12	13	14
15	16	17	18	19	20	21
22	23	24	25	26	27	28
29	30	31				

JUNE

S	M	T	W	T	F	S
			1	2	3	4
5	6	7	8	9	10	11
12	13	14	15	16	17	18
19	20	21	22	23	24	25
26	27	28	29	30		

JULY

S	M	T	W	T	F	S
					1	2
3	4	5	6	7	8	9
10	11	12	13	14	15	16
17	18	19	20	21	22	23
24	25	26	27	28	29	30
31						

AUGUST

S	M	T	W	T	F	S
	1	2	3	4	5	6
7	8	9	10	11	12	13
14	15	16	17	18	19	20
21	22	23	24	25	26	27
28	29	30	31			

SEPTEMBER

S	M	T	W	T	F	S
				1	2	3
4	5	6	7	8	9	10
11	12	13	14	15	16	17
18	19	20	21	22	23	24
25	26	27	28	29	30	

OCTOBER

S	M	T	W	T	F	S
						1
2	3	4	5	6	7	8
9	10	11	12	13	14	15
16	17	18	19	20	21	22
23	24	25	26	27	28	29
30	31					

NOVEMBER

S	M	T	W	T	F	S
	1	2	3	4	5	
6	7	8	9	10	11	12
13	14	15	16	17	18	19
20	21	22	23	24	25	26
27	28	29	30			

DECEMBER

S	M	T	W	T	F	S
				1	2	3
4	5	6	7	8	9	10
11	12	13	14	15	16	17
18	19	20	21	22	23	24
25	26	27	28	29	30	31

1989

JANUARY
S	M	T	W	T	F	S
1	2	3	4	5	6	7
8	9	10	11	12	13	14
15	16	17	18	19	20	21
22	23	24	25	26	27	28
29	30	31				

FEBRUARY
S	M	T	W	T	F	S
			1	2	3	4
5	6	7	8	9	10	11
12	13	14	15	16	17	18
19	20	21	22	23	24	25
26	27	28				

MARCH
S	M	T	W	T	F	S
			1	2	3	4
5	6	7	8	9	10	11
12	13	14	15	16	17	18
19	20	21	22	23	24	25
26	27	28	29	30	31	

APRIL
S	M	T	W	T	F	S
						1
2	3	4	5	6	7	8
9	10	11	12	13	14	15
16	17	18	19	20	21	22
23	24	25	26	27	28	29
30						

MAY
S	M	T	W	T	F	S
	1	2	3	4	5	6
7	8	9	10	11	12	13
14	15	16	17	18	19	20
21	22	23	24	25	26	27
28	29	30	31			

JUNE
S	M	T	W	T	F	S
				1	2	3
4	5	6	7	8	9	10
11	12	13	14	15	16	17
18	19	20	21	22	23	24
25	26	27	28	29	30	

JULY
S	M	T	W	T	F	S
						1
2	3	4	5	6	7	8
9	10	11	12	13	14	15
16	17	18	19	20	21	22
23	24	25	26	27	28	29
30	31					

AUGUST
S	M	T	W	T	F	S
		1	2	3	4	5
6	7	8	9	10	11	12
13	14	15	16	17	18	19
20	21	22	23	24	25	26
27	28	29	30	31		

SEPTEMBER
S	M	T	W	T	F	S
					1	2
3	4	5	6	7	8	9
10	11	12	13	14	15	16
17	18	19	20	21	22	23
24	25	26	27	28	29	30

OCTOBER
S	M	T	W	T	F	S
1	2	3	4	5	6	7
8	9	10	11	12	13	14
15	16	17	18	19	20	21
22	23	24	25	26	27	28
29	30	31				

NOVEMBER
S	M	T	W	T	F	S
			1	2	3	4
5	6	7	8	9	10	11
12	13	14	15	16	17	18
19	20	21	22	23	24	25
26	27	28	29	30		

DECEMBER
S	M	T	W	T	F	S
					1	2
3	4	5	6	7	8	9
10	11	12	13	14	15	16
17	18	19	20	21	22	23
24	25	26	27	28	29	30
31						

1990

JANUARY
S	M	T	W	T	F	S
	1	2	3	4	5	6
7	8	9	10	11	12	13
14	15	16	17	18	19	20
21	22	23	24	25	26	27
28	29	30	31			

FEBRUARY
S	M	T	W	T	F	S
				1	2	3
4	5	6	7	8	9	10
11	12	13	14	15	16	17
18	19	20	21	22	23	24
25	26	27	28			

MARCH
S	M	T	W	T	F	S
				1	2	3
4	5	6	7	8	9	10
11	12	13	14	15	16	17
18	19	20	21	22	23	24
25	26	27	28	29	30	31

APRIL
S	M	T	W	T	F	S
1	2	3	4	5	6	7
8	9	10	11	12	13	14
15	16	17	18	19	20	21
22	23	24	25	26	27	28
29	30					

MAY
S	M	T	W	T	F	S
		1	2	3	4	5
6	7	8	9	10	11	12
13	14	15	16	17	18	19
20	21	22	23	24	25	26
27	28	29	30	31		

JUNE
S	M	T	W	T	F	S
					1	2
3	4	5	6	7	8	9
10	11	12	13	14	15	16
17	18	19	20	21	22	23
24	25	26	27	28	29	30

JULY
S	M	T	W	T	F	S
1	2	3	4	5	6	7
8	9	10	11	12	13	14
15	16	17	18	19	20	21
22	23	24	25	26	27	28
29	30	31				

AUGUST
S	M	T	W	T	F	S
			1	2	3	4
5	6	7	8	9	10	11
12	13	14	15	16	17	18
19	20	21	22	23	24	25
26	27	28	29	30	31	

SEPTEMBER
S	M	T	W	T	F	S
						1
2	3	4	5	6	7	8
9	10	11	12	13	14	15
16	17	18	19	20	21	22
23	24	25	26	27	28	29
30						

OCTOBER
S	M	T	W	T	F	S
	1	2	3	4	5	6
7	8	9	10	11	12	13
14	15	16	17	18	19	20
21	22	23	24	25	26	27
28	29	30	31			

NOVEMBER
S	M	T	W	T	F	S
				1	2	3
4	5	6	7	8	9	10
11	12	13	14	15	16	17
18	19	20	21	22	23	24
25	26	27	28	29	30	

DECEMBER
S	M	T	W	T	F	S
						1
2	3	4	5	6	7	8
9	10	11	12	13	14	15
16	17	18	19	20	21	22
23	24	25	26	27	28	29
30	31					

1991

JANUARY
S	M	T	W	T	F	S
		1	2	3	4	5
6	7	8	9	10	11	12
13	14	15	16	17	18	19
20	21	22	23	24	25	26
27	28	29	30	31		

FEBRUARY
S	M	T	W	T	F	S
					1	2
3	4	5	6	7	8	9
10	11	12	13	14	15	16
17	18	19	20	21	22	23
24	25	26	27	28		

MARCH
S	M	T	W	T	F	S
					1	2
3	4	5	6	7	8	9
10	11	12	13	14	15	16
17	18	19	20	21	22	23
24	25	26	27	28	29	30
31						

APRIL
S	M	T	W	T	F	S
	1	2	3	4	5	6
7	8	9	10	11	12	13
14	15	16	17	18	19	20
21	22	23	24	25	26	27
28	29	30				

MAY
S	M	T	W	T	F	S
			1	2	3	4
5	6	7	8	9	10	11
12	13	14	15	16	17	18
19	20	21	22	23	24	25
26	27	28	29	30	31	

JUNE
S	M	T	W	T	F	S
						1
2	3	4	5	6	7	8
9	10	11	12	13	14	15
16	17	18	19	20	21	22
23	24	25	26	27	28	29
30						

JULY
S	M	T	W	T	F	S
	1	2	3	4	5	6
7	8	9	10	11	12	13
14	15	16	17	18	19	20
21	22	23	24	25	26	27
28	29	30	31			

AUGUST
S	M	T	W	T	F	S
				1	2	3
4	5	6	7	8	9	10
11	12	13	14	15	16	17
18	19	20	21	22	23	24
25	26	27	28	29	30	31

SEPTMEBER
S	M	T	W	T	F	S
1	2	3	4	5	6	7
8	9	10	11	12	13	14
15	16	17	18	19	20	21
22	23	24	25	26	27	28
29	30					

OCTOBER
S	M	T	W	T	F	S
		1	2	3	4	5
6	7	8	9	10	11	12
13	14	15	16	17	18	19
20	21	22	23	24	25	26
27	28	29	30	31		

NOVEMBER
S	M	T	W	T	F	S
					1	2
3	4	5	6	7	8	9
10	11	12	13	14	15	16
17	18	19	20	21	22	23
24	25	26	27	28	29	30

DECEMBER
S	M	T	W	T	F	S
1	2	3	4	5	6	7
8	9	10	11	12	13	14
15	16	17	18	19	20	21
22	23	24	25	26	27	28
29	30	31				

1992

JANUARY
S	M	T	W	T	F	S
			1	2	3	4
5	6	7	8	9	10	11
12	13	14	15	16	17	18
19	20	21	22	23	24	25
26	27	28	29	30	31	

FEBRUARY
S	M	T	W	T	F	S
						1
2	3	4	5	6	7	8
9	10	11	12	13	14	15
16	17	18	19	20	21	22
23	24	25	26	27	28	29

MARCH
S	M	T	W	T	F	S
1	2	3	4	5	6	7
8	9	10	11	12	13	14
15	16	17	18	19	20	21
22	23	24	25	26	27	28
29	30	31				

APRIL
S	M	T	W	T	F	S
			1	2	3	4
5	6	7	8	9	10	11
12	13	14	15	16	17	18
19	20	21	22	23	24	25
26	27	28	29	30		

MAY
S	M	T	W	T	F	S
					1	2
3	4	5	6	7	8	9
10	11	12	13	14	15	16
17	18	19	20	21	22	23
24	25	26	27	28	29	30
31						

JUNE
S	M	T	W	T	F	S
	1	2	3	4	5	6
7	8	9	10	11	12	13
14	15	16	17	18	19	20
21	22	23	24	25	26	27
28	29	30				

JULY
S	M	T	W	T	F	S
			1	2	3	4
5	6	7	8	9	10	11
12	13	14	15	16	17	18
19	20	21	22	23	24	25
26	27	28	29	30	31	

AUGUST
S	M	T	W	T	F	S
						1
2	3	4	5	6	7	8
9	10	11	12	13	14	15
16	17	18	19	20	21	22
23	24	25	26	27	28	29
30	31					

SEPTEMBER
S	M	T	W	T	F	S
		1	2	3	4	5
6	7	8	9	10	11	12
13	14	15	16	17	18	19
20	21	22	23	24	25	26
27	28	29	30			

OCTOBER
S	M	T	W	T	F	S
				1	2	3
4	5	6	7	8	9	10
11	12	13	14	15	16	17
18	19	20	21	22	23	24
25	26	27	28	29	30	31

NOVEMBER
S	M	T	W	T	F	S
1	2	3	4	5	6	7
8	9	10	11	12	13	14
15	16	17	18	19	20	21
22	23	24	25	26	27	28
29	30					

DECEMBER
S	M	T	W	T	F	S
		1	2	3	4	5
6	7	8	9	10	11	12
13	14	15	16	17	18	19
20	21	22	23	24	25	26
27	28	29	30	31		

Index

ABOUT THE AUTHOR

Emma J. Wisdom is a professional organizer who has planned hundreds of meetings for all types of groups, including family reunions. From an avid story writer as a child, acting in school plays, sales clerk, licensed hair stylist, certified professional secretary, speaker, to administrator and author, Wisdom has come full circle in search of her career niche.

A regular contributor to *Aim Magazine*, Wisdom has also written articles in other publications, bringing attention to such topics as office procedures, supervision, and women's issues.

Wisdom holds a degree from the University of Tennessee. She has held several professional and community affiliations, among which are included the American Society of Personnel Administration, Certified Professional Secretary Academy, National Association of Educational Office Personnel, Parents-Teachers Association, Nashville Symphony Guild, Middle Tennessee Genealogical Society, the National Writers Club, and National Advisory Board of *Today's Secretary*.

Her diverse experiences ultimately led her to write *A Practical Guide to Planning a Family Reunion*, which reflects her commitment to building and nurturing family relationships.

Born in Somerville, Texas, she has lived in North Carolina, Maryland, and New Jersey. She now resides in Nashville with her husband and their two college-age children.

FAMILY REUNION QUESTIONNAIRE

How often does your family have a family reunion?
_____ once a year _____ every other year _____other (specify)
_____

How long has your family been having reunions? _____ one year
_____ two years _____ five years _____ ten years _____
fifteen years _____ twenty years or more _____ other (specify)
_____

Where do you usually hold your reunion? _____ city of origin
_____different location each time _____ other (explain)
_____

How many days does your family reunion usually last? _____ one day
_____two days _____three days _____one week _____ longer
_____ other (specify) _____

What kind of activities do you usually have? (Describe. Use a separate sheet if necessary.)

What kinds of special or unique things do you do during your reunion to make it especially memorable? (Describe. Use a separate sheet if necessary.)

We'd appreciate your comments about your family or the book A PRACTICAL GUIDE TO PLANNING A FAMILY REUNION. Information will be shared with others interested in family reunion ideas.

Emma J. Wisdom

TO ORDER

Clip and return to:

Post Oak Publications
Post Office Box 8455
Nashville, Tennessee 37207-0455

Please send _____ copies @ $8.95 each of *A PRACTICAL GUIDE TO PLANNING A FAMILY REUNION* by Emma J. Wisdom

___ Check Enclosed. Add $2.00 for postage and handling for first book and $0.50 for each additional book (Tennessee residents add 7 3/4% sales tax).

Name _____

Address _____

City _____ State _____ Zip _____

Allow 4-6 weeks for delivery

===

TO ORDER

Clip and return to:

Post Oak Publications
Post Office Box 8455
Nashville, Tennessee 37207-0455

Please send _____ copies @ $8.95 each of *A PRACTICAL GUIDE TO PLANNING A FAMILY REUNION* by Emma J. Wisdom

___ Check Enclosed. Add $2.00 for postage and handling for first book and $0.50 for each additional book (Tennessee residents add 7 3/4% sales tax).

Name _____

Address _____

City _____ State _____ Zip _____

Allow 4-6 weeks for delivery